NOT so ORDINARY
DEVOTIONAL PICTURE BOOK

Special Thanks

Travis Bookout, Tom Larkin, David Dunaway, Molly Turner and Dale Pollard

Not So Ordinary

Text Copyright 2022

Illustration Copyright 2022

All Rights Reserved. Printed in the United States of America

ISBN: 978-1-952955-35-8

Kaio Publications

www.kaiopublications.org

Each spread of this book contains accounts of Bible characters that demonstrate God using ordinary people in order to accomplish extraordinary things. It is important that ALL of God's children, even the smallest ones, have material they can enjoy and relate to in order to grow into the Christians the world needs.

ELIJAH & THE WIDOW

Travis Bookout

The Bible says Elijah was "a man with a nature like ours" (James 5:17). This means he didn't have superpowers. He was not the strongest, smartest, or most special person alive. He was a person just like you and me, but God used him to do incredible things. He stood up against evil kings, he performed miracles, and he raised someone back to life.

There was a widow from Sidon who had one son. Being a widow meant her husband had died. Living in Sidon meant she was not from Israel and was a Gentile. Being a woman meant she didn't have the opportunity to work and make money like a man. She loved her son very much and he would take care of her. Sadly, one day, her son died.

After this happened, she came to Elijah. Elijah put the boy on his bed, laid down on the boy three times, and begged God, "Let this child's life come into him again" (1 Kings 17:21). God listened and lovingly brought the boy back to life. His mother was so happy and thankful. She trusted that Elijah was a true prophet of God.

MOSES
Dale Pollard

A LoNNNnnnNnNnNnnng time ago in the sun roasted land of Egypt lived a man named Moses. Nobody knows if his friends called him "Moe" but that is a pretty good nickname. Moses had parents with strange names like "Amram" (sounds like "ham slam") and Jochebed.

Moses was a hero! Sort of. He didn't always act like a hero. He had difficulty controlling his anger. There were times in his life where he would become so mad he would almost explode! On at least one occasion, Moses was filled with such rage that he killed an Egyptian man. Another time he threw a giant stone called "The Ten Commandments" off a mountain! Then there was the day God told him to speak to a rock, and if he did, water would come pouring out. At that time Moses and all of his people were really thirsty because they were in the desert, and it's hard to find water in a sandy place like a desert. Instead of listening to God's command to talk to the rock, Moses smacks the rock with his walking stick.

But, Moses was a hero! Well, kind of. He really didn't sound like a hero. Maybe he had a stutter? Maybe he couldn't say his "R"s very well? Nobody knows. But, Moses was still a hero! Well, pretty much. He really didn't look like a hero. He was an old man when he began leading his people in the desert.

But... Moses was a hero? The man who was born in the sun roasted land of Egypt, whose friends could have called him Moe, and had parents with strange names? The man who didn't always act like a hero? Or sound like a hero? Or even look like a hero? HOW IS HE A HERO?! Moses did big things because God helped him do big things. Everybody can do big things if they let God help! YOU will do BIG things when you let God help.

GIDEON
David Dunaway

"Last again" Mikey said to himself. He loved playing ball at recess, but he was always the last one picked. Mikey was not the tallest of kids nor was he good at sports like others. Many times, he was the one who messed up and maybe even cost his team the game. He still loved to play. It would be nice to not be the last one picked someday.

There was a soldier of the children of Israel, before kings ruled the nation whose name was Gideon. Even though Gideon was a soldier, in many ways, he was similar to Mikey. He was not the first person you would choose to lead a battle against a big, fierce nation of bad guys.

The Midianites were the bad guys. They were bullies. The children of Israel had to hide in the mountains and in caves. It was a hard time, but it was time for God to pick a leader to save His people.

An angel from God came to Gideon one night while he was working. The angel said Gideon was a "mighty man of valor" and that God had chosen him to lead the battle against the Midianites. Gideon was not used to that praise and recognition, but he loved serving God, so Gideon put his trust in Him.

Gideon assembled an army of thousands of soldiers to fight the Midianites, but God said there were too many. God reduced Gideon's army from thousands to just 300 soldiers, and with God and those soldiers the bad guys were defeated.

God will help us overcome big stuff in our lives. We have to trust Him. Sometimes it doesn't look the way we think it should, and it's scary. We need to understand that God has plans for us, and it doesn't take a good ball player or someone who is tall or fast. God uses our uniqueness to do amazing things.

Maid in Naaman's House
Tom Larkin

Being kind is always the right thing to do. The little maid had been a servant for Naaman's wife since she had been kidnapped from her Israelite home. How sad and afraid she must have been when she was taken from her family! As a slave in Syria, she lived in the home of an important soldier. Though he was a leper, Naaman was a great captain in the army of Syria. Even though the little maid had been taken from her home and family, she was polite and courteous to her mistress.

She was concerned about the health of her master Naaman. She even wished that he was with the prophet in Samaria so that he could be healed. And because of her kindness, Naaman was healed and his life was saved! And, even more importantly, he learned the truth about God.

Sometimes we are mistreated by others. It is never right for that to happen, but the way we respond is important. The way we respond says something about the kind of people we are. The Bible tells us to be kind even when we are being mistreated. It tells us to overcome evil by being good. When we are good to those who mistreat us, we are being like God. This helps others learn about God. And, like Naaman, they may decide to live their lives for him.

Years later, King Josiah began repairing the temple because the people had not used it in a long time to worship God. During these repairs, Hilkiah, the high priest, found a copy of God's law in the temple. Josiah was so sad when he heard what was in the law that he tore his clothes and wept because he knew that they had not been doing what the Law said.

Josiah sent the high priest to a prophetess named Huldah. She told him that God would judge His people because of their sins. If Josiah humbled himself before God, he would not see this judgment, but would go to his Father's in peace.

Josiah called the people together and read God's law to them. He promised to keep God's law, and the people agreed. They promised to obey God with all of their heart and soul. They began doing this by keeping the Passover feast just like the law commanded.

Even though you are young, just like Josiah, you can love God with all of your heart and obey his word.

MATTHEW

David Dunaway

Have you ever been asked to do something that is not popular? It may be at home or at school. The task may be something that makes others laugh at you or make fun of you. Something never done by the popular kids. Not every task in life is what we would call fun or popular.

Jesus chose twelve men to do a special task for Him. This task would not always be fun or popular. In fact, a lot of the time it would be dangerous. There was a man who dealt with unpopular tasks every day—Matthew, the tax collector.

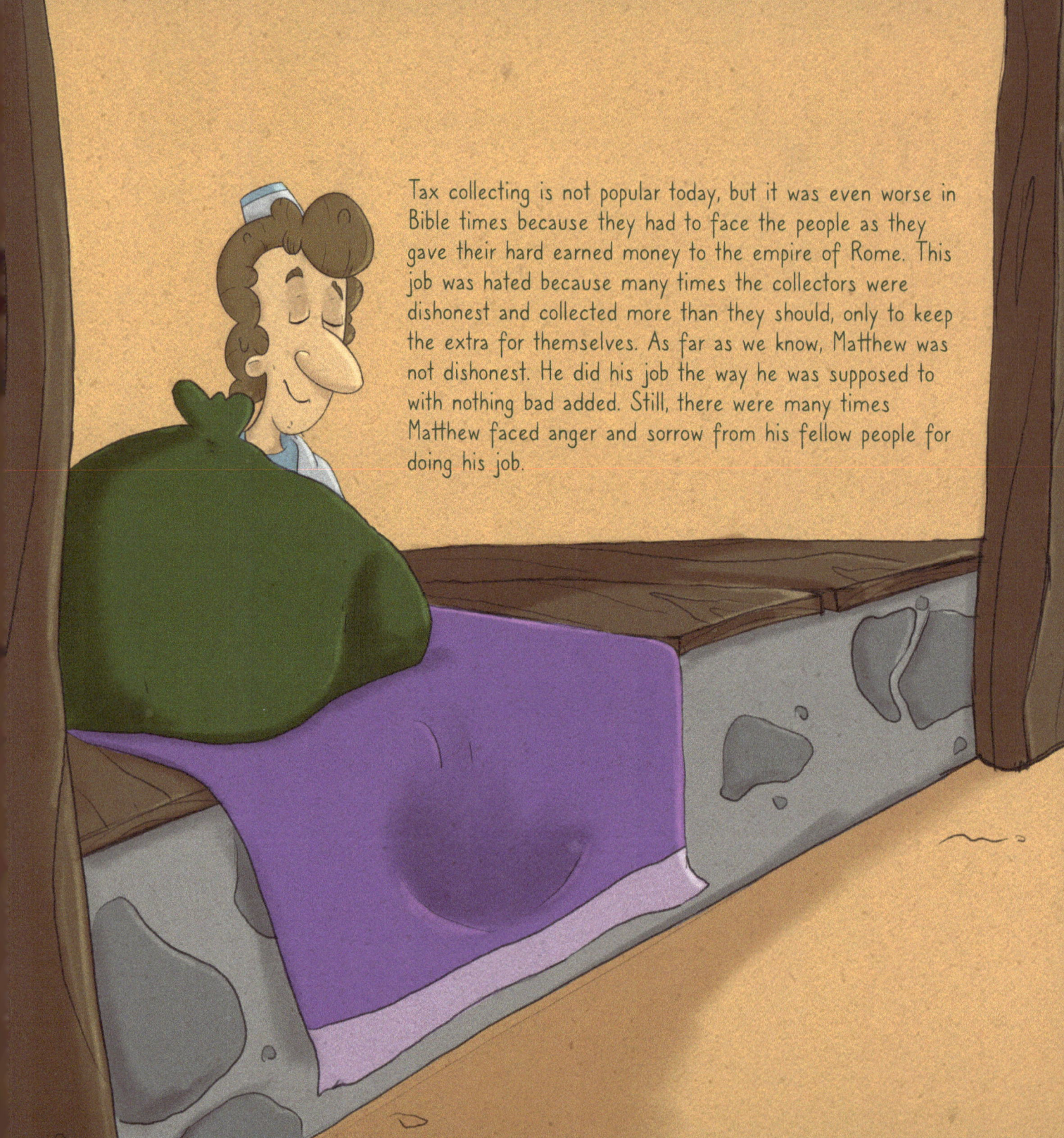

Tax collecting is not popular today, but it was even worse in Bible times because they had to face the people as they gave their hard earned money to the empire of Rome. This job was hated because many times the collectors were dishonest and collected more than they should, only to keep the extra for themselves. As far as we know, Matthew was not dishonest. He did his job the way he was supposed to with nothing bad added. Still, there were many times Matthew faced anger and sorrow from his fellow people for doing his job.

Jesus chose Matthew because he would do the task the right way no matter how unpopular. Teaching about the way to get to heaven is a great thing. Not all people want to hear it now, and it was true during Matthew's time. Today, there may be things you are asked to do around the house or at school that may not be fun or popular, but if you do it the right way, you will always know you are pleasing God.

Jesus taught that the most important things in the world are to love God and to love your neighbor. One day someone challenged Jesus, asking, "And who is my neighbor?" (Luke 10:29). This man only wanted neighbors who lived near him, believed like him, and were part of his country, Israel. He did not want to love anyone else.

Jesus answered with a story about a man who was beaten up by robbers. He was hurt so badly he couldn't get off the ground. Then two Israelites, a priest and a Levite, walked right past him and didn't help or care. But a third person walked by who was a Samaritan. The Samaritans were not neighbors, but enemies, of Israel. They didn't live in the same place or share the same beliefs. However, this Samaritan still helped. He picked up the injured man, took him somewhere safe, and paid for everything he needed.

This Samaritan showed compassion to someone who was different. He loved his enemy and was a true neighbor. Jesus tells us to "Go, and do likewise" (Luke 10:37). Jesus wants us to be kind and help people, to love even our enemies, and to be a neighbor to everyone.

There is a story in the Bible about a woman named Dorcas. Dorcas was a very giving and selfless woman, much like Mrs. Joyce. The Bible says Dorcas was "full of good works and acts of charity." She was always helping people in need by making clothes for those who did not have any and by praying for the people around her. When Dorcas died, one of Jesus's followers, Peter, was in a town nearby. Two of the other disciples heard Peter was close to Dorcas's home and asked for him to visit Dorcas. Peter went to her home right away. When he got there, he saw many of her friends crying because of her passing. He asked the people to go outside, and he knelt down beside Dorcas, prayed for her, and said "arise!" Immediately, her eyes opened, and she sat up.

It makes God very happy when we help people. Whether that person is a friend or a stranger, we can do our best to help them. It can be as simple as giving some of your old clothes to the homeless shelter. We can always find a way to give to others, no matter what their needs may be.

The Bible tells us of many times when God used his people to do extraordinary things. The people in the Bible made a huge difference in the world around them by obeying God, healing people or simply being kind to others. BUT today God needs someone else. **GOD NEEDS YOU!**

You may not think you are the strongest, fastest or bravest person, and you might not be, but God has a plan. He will use ordinary kids just like you to do some awesome things! Trust in God, believe He has a job for you to do, and pray that you will do the right thing. You might just find out you are Not So Ordinary after all!